6—

# ARK

Ed Madden

SIBLING RIVALRY PRESS
LITTLE ROCK, ARKANSAS
DISTURB / ENRAPTURE

Ark

Copyright © 2016 by Ed Madden

Cover art: *Alien Child* by Carroll Cloar. Hirshhorn Museum and Sculpture Garden, Smithsonian Institution, Gift of Joseph H. Hirshhorn, 1966. Photographer: Cathy Carver.

Author photo by Forrest Clonts
Cover design by Seth Pennington

Sibling Rivalry Press, LLC
PO Box 26147
Little Rock, AR 72221

info@siblingrivalrypress.com

www.siblingrivalrypress.com

ISBN: 978-1-943977-08-6

Library of Congress Control No: 2015960257

This title is housed permanently in the Library of Congress Rare Books and Special Collections Vault.

First Sibling Rivalry Press Edition, March 2016

Home was the center of the world because it was the place where a vertical line crossed with a horizontal one. The vertical line was a path leading upwards to the sky and downwards to the underworld. The horizontal line represented the traffic of the world, all the possible roads leading across the earth to other places.

– John Berger, *And Our Faces, My Heart, Brief as Photos*

The size of sorrow is the size of my father.

– Frank McGuinness, *Booterstown*

# CONTENTS

## III – In my father's house

# ARK

*Christmas 1966*

The small box is filled with little beasts—
a barn that's a barge, a boat—the ark's

ridged sides like boards, a plastic plank,
a deck that drops in fitted slots, but lifted

reveals that zoo of twos—heaped beasts
to be released beneath a glittering tree,

its dove-clipped limbs. Dad's asleep
in his reclining seat, and crumpled waves

of paper recede as Mom circles the room.
The humming wheel throws light across the walls.

# - I -

## ADRIFT

# ADRIFT OFF THE ISLETS OF LANGERHANS

Sails down, we drift. Hospital time, fluid.
The room feels unmoored, floating world.

The horizon is a flotilla of hospitals:
Aunt Mary Etta names them one by one.

One night the moon loomed over them, a cold sun.
One day, a hawk pursued by two crows.

Signals flicker the inlets, like lightning that night,
followed by floods, followed by darkness.

*Pancreas*, meaning sweetbread, from the Greek
*pan* for all, from the Greek *kreas*, flesh.

The sign in the hall says: *Quiet, Please, Healing in Progress.*

An island of silence, like the quiet we've tended
for years, cultivating the rift between us.

*Adeno*, meaning gland, derived from the Greek for acorn.
All flesh meaning without cartilage or bone.

We sail beneath the sign of the crab,
though the sky says otherwise: ram and bull.

## LAST NIGHT

Last night, bright moon,
dark trees lining each horizon,

armadillo digging up the flowerbed.
The yucca's last buds glow white.

Last night, a nightmare, lame,
as nightmares come, but

for all that, I woke up calling out
for my father's help. My mother

woke, her soft feet at the door.

Last night, she says, she heard voices,
in the house, outside the window,

someone calling her name.
It's like that now.

Last night my dad asked how I got there,
sitting beside his bed, his head

against the rail, his soft focus stare.
He says something now I can't quite hear,

his quiet voice receding, distant,
another room. My mom says sometimes

he waves at someone, but no one's there.

# FLOOD

*March 2011*

To the south, the ditch is out, the field
awash with brown water, white in morning light, the horizon

a furred ridge of dark green trees
that traces the turn of drowned banks, the line and curve

of Remmel Ditch. All around the waters rising—
the Cache, the White, the Black, Bayou De View—and on the news,

sandbags in Jacksonport, Pocahontas, Paragould,
roads washed out, the interstate closed. Aunt Elaine shows us photos

on her phone of the levee around her house,
sandbagged circles at every door, the porch. The road west,

our way out, is under water too,
though tractors or a jacked-up four-wheel-drive truck get through,

flooded to just beyond there where
the old Stitt house used to be, its dooryard garden now

clumps of damp jonquils bloomed out
and brown, a sodden lot of weeds and grass, thick-stitched with vetch.

The postman won't come through it, the flag
on the box up three days now, and we have to drive out

to pick up the hospice nurse, her little car
parked off the blacktop a mile away. On the way back,

I see a coot swimming in the field, a flourish
of blackbirds swerving along the road's washed-out shoulder,

and when I park, in the backyard, we can hear
the dove that lives there, above us, in the pines, asking,

*who—oh who who who?*

# AFTER LONG SILENCE

My father is a puzzle box. He's a map folded up.

The nurse says he has something to tell me.
He stares at me, but never tells me.

My mother is a vase tipped over.
Daylilies bloom one day, and each day is another.

So many vases left after her accident,
stacked in the closet, like empty wrappers, like magic.

My father is a shrunken head and a blanket.
*What do you want to say, old man, that you haven't said already?*

Outside, a skunk or something shuffling on the carport, the light is on.

My father is a box of lamentations, unsaid.
My mother is a blue jar.

Listen: my mother's soft snoring, the daylilies furled in the dark.

# BRIDGE

Over dinner
at On the Border,
Uncle Rick says
*it's all water*
*under the bridge*
*now* about
his own dad, dead
a decade. Mom's flipping
the menu, some quip
about getting past
the liquor to find the food,
and I wonder
what he meant, though
I know something
of the bitterness
back then. When we get
home days later,
I discover the old
river bridge—fallen in
all those years—
is rebuilt, scribbled
with teen graffiti.
My folks no longer live
on a dead end
road. Every day, someone
brings food. After a week
or so, we throw
old casseroles
in the ditch, watch
the sweet rotten flotsam
drift away.

# RABBIT

A rabbit sits still
as they will to hide
in plain sight, its black eyes
wide and watching
me. The yard is riddled
with armadillo digs,
its burrow under
the quince—we can't
get rid of it, though
we try. We'll have
to sit up some night
with a gun.

My dad's inside,
twisting in the dark
drift of sleep. I hear
frogsong and mockingbird,
the low gurgle at the road
where a bridge constricts
the flooded ditch, its banks
hidden in the sheet of silt
and wave that washes
the fields. When
I step close, the rabbit
twists into a thicket
of honeysuckle at the fence.
I killed a snake there
last week as it slid out
beneath my feet, like
death, too near.

## HIS BOOTS

Dress boots rest on the mudroom sink,
ready for a polish, I think—black
and silver-stitched Western style,
the toe flower a flourish of loops,

infinite, above the sharp Nocona toe—
ready to be packed with a suit,
a tie. I need to clean them, buff them
up, not sure how long I've got

to get them ready for the journey,
the one he's just begun—getting
ready in the bedroom down
the hall, talking about his daddy,

talking about his brothers, talking
about his dead brothers.

# FIST

The leaves on the lawn are brown.
Beneath them, the wet ground.

Beneath them, the silver roots.
Beneath them, the darkness.

Given the chance to change,
you hold on, the fist

a clenched bulb.
Last year's tulips come up again,

smaller, shorter, failing—
the stunted stem a symptom.

The rain tastes like copper,
an old coin on the tongue.

Across the yard, the poppies
have reseeded themselves—

sharp filigree of bright green.

# FIELD GUIDE, AFTER THE FLOODS

I.

In March, when we got the diagnosis, drove him home,
there were redbuds in bloom along the road,

out back where the barn fell,
in the front yard, covered with poison ivy we can't kill,

and buckeyes coming up along the ditch, shoots
like red fingers, new leaves red as bruises,

and dock leaves along the road like tongues.

II.

Where the Stitt house used to be: hyacinth, vetch,
and everywhere dead nettle.

At the woodpile: leather flower. Under the cypress:
   dayflower.

Out back: henbit and wood sorrel,
cut-leaved primrose, skullcap, dog fennel.

III.

In the fields, buttercup and vetch as the floods receded,
and later, as the plows began their business, something we'd
   never seen:

bear tracks. My cousin took a photo on his phone.
Days later, the newspaper reported two bears hit and killed on
   local roads.

# TROUBLING THE WATER

*after John 5 :4*

I.

A gallinule walks on water, walks across
a thick mat of straw, what's left, what's lost, the stalks,
the threshed and thrown, the wind

raking the waves, raking it all to that corner of the flooded field, ripples
of grey water and straw, dead stuff, a bird.
This was before. This was when

I went out in the old truck to pick up the nurse
at the highway. She wasn't sure about all the water, left her car.
This was before. In the book of healings,

there's something perverse about that angel,
the one at the pool, watching the crowd, the crippled and halt, withered,
impotent, blind, all of them waiting for that first sign of trouble,

a ripple, like a finger dipped
in the water—and then that shuffling, a mass of the desperate
mobilized—*first one in, wins*—the others stuck

at the edge of it, some of them wet
but sicker for having just missed it, the miracle,
watching it, watching him, the one who made it, and in the back,

the one who never does.

II.

*Sir, I have no man, when the water is troubled, to put me into the pool.*
I lift my dad to his wheelchair. We go out
to the carport so he can smoke while the nurse

changes his bed, gets his bath ready, the cloths and basin
of water, the mouth swabs, the microwave shampoo cap.
This was before. Later versions

leave out the angel, leave out the troubling of the water,
just a pool near the sheep market,
sick people at the edge.

In the book of healings—*all these goddamn healings*—
the guy finally gets it, healing, picks up his bed,
and walks. I leave my dad in his chair

for the nurse to start his bath.

# - II -

# LANDSCAPE, WITH LEVEES

# THE HOUSE AND THE SURROUNDING FIELDS

Here, he stood here, at the foot
of the dirt road. The house lifted

above the fields like a boat. The fields
grew dark. The sky emptied itself

of whatever was once there.

The house glowed, pole star, the fields
and stubbled rows tilting round it. Was he

leaving? Was he returning? The house tilted
above the fields like an ark resting,

at last, here, in the brown fields,

the dove and crow long gone, the road
like an itch, like a brown ribbon,

and him doing what he had to do.

# HOME

Putting stuff away suggests I'll stay—
at least a bit, as if it's no longer
the short visit I'd intended, but something
more, as it must be now. In a hotel,
I fill the drawers first thing, but here
I'd resisted it, wanted to be ready
to go—clothes stacked on a chair, near
the door, wheelchair and unused bedside commode
parked in my room, best place for them I'd said,
near enough to his room, not in my way,
their own big bed shoved in my brother's room
to make way for hospital stuff, the tank
and tubes, the railed bed, a twin for my mom
rolled in beside. My room is my own,
the one I grew up in, my bed gone,
instead an antique bed for guests, metal
headboard like a giant crib. Most
of my old books are gone, but the shelves
are still haunted, like the mirror, the closet,
the curtains closed to the road—the blades
of memory could be anywhere, rusty
and sharp, even here in the bathroom cabinet,
where I tuck my own soap, drugs
for the hypertension I inherit.
　　　　　　　　　　　By now
I know where the mugs are, can start the coffee
when I get up, long before they wake,
have the schedule down for when he takes
his meds—my cell phone set for five, the one
we might forget. It's almost nine, I've drunk
half a pot, it's almost time to wash
my hands in hot water, dry on paper
towel, fill a plastic cup with filtered

water, and count out the morning meds.
It's how the day begins. Outside the kitchen
window, the rabbit's back, unafraid.
When I walk out, it pauses. It doesn't run.
Hungry, it turns back to the rain-washed lawn.

# INSTRUCTIONS

1.

Make sure he swallows them all.
Ask if he needs another sip of water.

Ask if he's okay before he drifts
back to sleep. He will sleep a lot.

Brush his hair over as he sleeps.
His face is thin now, that spot

over his eye darker, the one he got
from Grandpa Roy. His hands seem

large and dark against his thin frame,
clasped over his chest in the dim room.

2.

When he wakes, ask if he's okay.
If he says something that makes

no sense, just say okay.
*Did you miss the bus?* No,

I'm staying with you today.
*Do we need to put a battery*

*on that tractor?* No, but you need
to finish taking your medicine.

*How long are you going to be here?*
Till you're okay.

# MY FATHER AS *FANTASTIC VOYAGE* (1966)


He lies in the hospital bed like Jan Benes, and we know the crew
has to get in and fix him. So much depends on this. No Raquel,

just my mom, her neck bent from the accident, her hair pinned
back when we've got a job to do. And I can't decide who

I am—Dr. Duval, who lasers the clot, would be spot on,
but more likely Charles Grant, secret agent, played by

Stephen Boyd, Irishman from Antrim, known best as Messala in the classic
*Ben-Hur*, Ben's best friend, playing opposite Charleton Heston

as Hur himself, who later denied rumors of the gay subtext
in the script, though Boyd was in on it to the hilt, played up

the scorned love of Hess as Hur. Dr. Michaels, played by
Donald Pleasence, is the enemy within—a Brit. We remember

the crashed ship and the white blood cells eating him at the end
of the film, but he's still there. My mom says there's a demon inside

my dad, and Pleasence played Satan the year before in *The Greatest Story
Ever Told*, and later Pontius Pilate in *The Passover Plot*

and Dr. Loomis in *Halloween*. The next year, Welch wore a fur
bikini in *One Million Years B.C.* I was three.

And Boyd played Nimrod, defied God as Babel-builder in *The Bible:
In the Beginning*. And just before he died, he played Father

Costigan, Irish terrorist turned pretend priest and gunrunner
on *Hawaii Five-O*, one isle to another. Our crew is small.

We navigate the Islets of Langerhans. The journey in is not easy.
I brush back his hair when I wake him for his meds, hold

the straw at his lips, imagine the pill at the back of his throat,
wish him to swallow, not cough, lean in as if I could steer it in,

make the pills work. I watch him grimace at the taste of it,
as he swallows, hard, his throat tightening, then released.

The first pill down, just six to go.

# EASY

We ask each day what you're hungry for,
try Loretta's roast, some chicken, corn
and peas. A few bites, you're through, unless
we say there's cake. Mom kept ice cream
in the hospital fridge; now everyone brings
things we know you'll eat—Betty's coconut
pie or Ronda's lemon icebox, Aunt Elaine's
strawberry cake (its icing a thick sludge
of butter, strawberries, sugar, cream cheese).
Uncle Ken drops by with fried pies
from M.J.'s, says he knows you like the peach.

When the apples we'd overbought were going
bad, Suzanne stopped by with a recipe for easy
apple dumplings and stuff to make it, crescent
rolls, sugar, a can of Mountain Dew—
Mom pops the top, pours it over
the whole pan of wrapped and sugared apples,
when she's through, slides it in the oven.

On TV we see people losing homes,
roads closed, rivers flooding, a tornado
somewhere, near—the local news, but elsewhere
a royal wedding, froth of gown and gossip.
My first day back, you asked about *your mate*,
referred to Romans 1, but now we've settled
into something new—not easy, but less
of all that stuff about choice and sin,
the how and when of why we didn't talk
for so long back then. I sit beside the bed,
we eat apple dumplings, watch TV,
saying nothing, just eating something easy.

# HOW TO LIFT HIM

Don't pick him up by the pits,
which seems easiest. You risk

broken bones, bruised skin.
Instead, once he's eased up, sits,

shoulders hunched, feet slung
over the edge, lean down for the hug,

your arms under his and around,
hands flat against his back, his arms around

you. This is what you do. Then lift him,
his feet between yours, this timid

dance around, this turn. Tell him
to bend his knees as you ease him

down to the chair, its wheels locked,
set him in slow. Kneel in front

as if to receive his blessing.

Lift each foot to its rest. Wrap
a blanket around him—you're going out.

Stop at the old flat-front desk,
last hiding place for his cigarettes—

why he wanted up, after all. Stop
at the edge of the porch and lock

the wheels. Make sure he's in the sun.
Stand silent by, he won't talk much,

though the lonely cat will,
rubbing its back against the wheels.

# SNAKE

Black snake's a thick
cursive on the road,
sliding yardward.
Dad's smoking in his chair,
says *grab the shovel.*
I do as I'm told,
chop its neck
against the gravel
as it flashes white
and bites the air.

Days before,
a grass snake like
a thin vine tendrilled
the shovel handle
on the porch,
green and slow.
The cat ignored it,
I let it go.

# DEAD ZONES

Cellphone dead zones
roam my parent's home—
any room can have one.

Sometimes you have to stand
at a window, a particular
wall. Sometimes you'll go

to the front porch,
the wide southern sky
all around—or the carport,

open east and west—
and still no service, no sound.
Some nights, Dad reminds us

of the dead—they're
on his mind, they visit,
his dead brothers.

"Have you seen Dale yet?"
He leans across the bed,
tells me, "Help me

remember to call
Ralph tomorrow."
He tells my mom,

"I've got your daddy's
address if you want
to sign a card for him."

# BLACK TAPE

1.

Three or four lines that look alike run thru the attic.
Only your brother knows which one will connect.

He knows by trial and error.

Start with error.

2.

Take into consideration the fact
that the distance across the house is lengthened considerably

by the railings on your father's bed.

Take into consideration the history of antennae—
rabbit ears, roof mounts, the dish—

the history here of poor reception.

3.

Your brother is in the attic.

When he tugs on the right line, call out.

Use black tape to tape it to the wall, so he'll know,
so he can make the connection, later.

# RESEMBLANCES

*I. Going through photos with my mom*

What I lost, after all,
was not, was never
there, I never knew
how they grew, or if
they knew enough
to know I wasn't
there. Strange uncle,
somewhere.

These photos she shows—
nephews and niece, known
now but not then, when,
as she shows but never
tells, they were there,
but not me.

We open the albums: I try
to pick the moment
I'm gone for good,
or not, as now a nephew
nestles in a stack, and
I'm sure it's my brother,
my niece my mother, the way
faces ghost each other,
like mine, there,
among them.

## II. Hyacinths, Star-of-Bethlehem

The blue flowers he says are wild
are not quite, just escaped, marked
an old yard, scraped by plow
to bank, edge of field. They ruffle
up the green mound of leaves
where he tucked them in the lawn,
in the shade beneath the trees.

Her periwinkles are not that
either, but white and simple, like
winking stars splayed among the faded
jonquils, and really little lilies
though a gift all the same,
despite the name.

I wasn't here for years, heard
what he said and wrote—insistent
note read and reread, recalled
his voice that one visit when
he said *we will never,*
the blah blah of law, the lord,
*your choice,* difficulties of love
and such. For all that, still
I sit beside his bed, sit near,
for all that's the past, when
back then— but now
I'm here.

# LANDSCAPE, WITH LEVEES

*"If this is the middle, how long does it last?"*
Luisa A. Igloria

Yesterday, they put up levees in the field
across the road, the new rice a green sheen,
the levees ready for what's to come.
When I drive to town, I leave the windows
down, drink in the smell of well water,
metallic, cold. We think we've been close,
but can't know. That weekend he was away
from us, his eyes glazed and moving around
the room, his hands picking at the blanket,
his feet twitching, jerking beneath the sheets.
That morning he couldn't breathe.

Since I've been here, the floods have receded
from the fields, the men and tractors taken
over—landplanes leveled the field for the coming
rows, a red Case IH and a huge
John Deere pulling the yellow planes,
the long silver blades across the field.
Disk and plow have turned stubble under,
and weeds, the trees along the ditch filled out
thick and green. The river stalled a while,
so much water coming down the ditch
it ran backward for two days, but that's passed.

The nurse blames the moon for dad's moods,
says there was a solar eclipse the day
he decided to die, though all his vital signs
were fine. That night he said goodbye, leaned back
in bed, and waited. Nothing happened, and he was
mad, the next morning, that he hadn't
been taken. *I'm still here?* Outside we could hear
the tractors starting on another field.

# WHEN MY FATHER WOKE

When my father woke, he called out,
and my mother rose from her bed,
asked him what he wanted, said
she was there. I was at the door.

When my father woke, he called out,
and I heard him from the kitchen,
lingering over my coffee, having
fed the cat, having eaten my oatmeal,

having watched the birds beneath
the kitchen window, the fidget
and dither of three-lined sparrows
flipping through the dead leaves.

When my father woke, he called out,
and my mother rose from her bed,
quickly, never knowing, asked him
what he wanted, said she was there.

Sometimes it took a moment for him
to reply. Sometimes it was urgent.
Sometimes he was hungry.

When my father woke, he called out,
and sometimes I was there before
my mother woke, doing what
he needed to be done.

When my father woke, he called out,
and my mother rose from her bed,
coming to his side, like the sun
lifting in the east, and the day

began, revolving around him,
and we hovered near his bed
in our small orbits, our small
impermanent orbits.

# SONG

The day my father didn't die was gray,
a gray Sunday, the lower fields a plain
of mud and dark water. The mercury sank.
It was dark and cold. He was ready
to go. Coyotes quibbled the night before,
but by morning just the cat, hungry
on the porch. All day that day, a mockingbird
sang—we could hear it inside the house,
in his room, over the oxygen, its bubbles
and pump. I went outside for a moment, stood
beneath the tree, listening, trying to put
words to the song. No words came.
The bird kept singing.

# RAIN

Nothing to watch but the rain,
the way it fogs the field
this afternoon.

The house quiet, visitors gone,
so now it's just my mom
and me, my dad,

asleep for now in the railed bed.
From the porch I watch
the slow rain.

It's not that I want to not
be here, not that, no.
It's just that

I want to be a rock
in the unfinished walk,
to be wet

and cold, to be the wet road
going nowhere, going anywhere
through the rain.

## COLD

My father is looking at a spot near the door.
*Get him a blanket.*

Who?
*The little boy, over there, on the floor.*

*He's cold.*
The sun comes in the window,

polishes the bedrails,
a lily's glossy leaves on the dresser.

Okay. Are you cold, too?
*Maybe.*

I'll get you another blanket too.
*Okay, but don't forget the little boy.*

# BECAUSE

Vince the physical therapist tells my dad the reason he's here is because he represses his emotions. The latest issue of *Christian Woman* tells my mom a boy is gay because he doesn't relate to his father. The nurse says my dad won't take his meds because it's all he can control, so he says *no*.

Vince tells him, Everyone I know that's got your cancer doesn't show their emotions. The Christian mom, penname Anonymous, who wrote about her son, calls it SSA—same-sex attraction, the letters a label, an illness too long or shocking to name. I tell my dad I know he's mad, but the pills won't keep him from dying (he's ready to go), just stop the pain. He still says *no*.

Vince tells my dad, There's things you've been through, and you've just tried to suffer with it. You've been tough. (I wonder if he includes me in the list of *what you've been through*.) Anonymous in the latest *Christian Woman* says parents can't be solely to blame, but "they should be aware of the need to instill their children with proper gender identity." My cousin asks me if I've been out in the fields to drive a tractor since I've been home, and if I miss it. (I say no.)

Vince says, The only way for you to get over this is for you to start showing your emotions. Anonymous says a boy may have a personality so different from his father's that he doesn't relate well, causing the boy to relate more to the mother. Dad tells me to tell my mom he needs something to eat.

Vince tells my dad to watch some sad movies because he needs to cry. *Christian Woman* says same-sex attraction is "an emotional need to overcome a relational deficit." My mom tells me today that if I hadn't been here, she'd have had to put him in a nursing home, she couldn't handle it.

Vince quotes Proverbs, a merry heart is medicine, but a weary heart dries the bones. *Christian Woman* says, "While my husband and I grieve for what must have occurred to create the SSA in our child, we are more concerned for his future." I tell my dad, I don't need to be here if you're not taking your meds—that's why I'm here, to help. He says no, eyes closed, but reaches to hold my hand.

# FOOTNOTE ON THE ISLETS OF LANGERHANS

Months before my arrival, field mice left a nest
of acorns under a comforter on the guest bed.

Acorns also between the cushions of the blue couch.
*Adeno*, meaning gland, derived from the Greek for acorn.

My father is talking in his sleep in the next room.

Paul Langerhans was only twenty-two when he discovered
the islets that bear his name—1869, a year of discovery:

Islets of Langerhans, periodic table, vacuum, homosexual.
*Uncinate*, meaning bent at the end like a hook, unciform.

His strange heart, the unbranched artery compensating
for the dark skies, cold rain on the day he didn't die.

Every morning I measure out his meds.

Soak sweetbreads in cold water first to remove the blood.
Use your fingers to remove visible veins and gristle.

I wake early one dark morning, hearing a mouse
in the closet, rolling an acorn across the floor.

The islets are manufacturing plants, busy producing insulin.
These are the flowers that bloom on the islands:

tuber omentale, lesser omentum, omental bursa,
pylorus, duodenum, the ampulla of Vater.

*Ampulla* meaning flask, a small bottle used for ointment,
holy water, holy oil, something for anointing.

My father in the next room, talking in his sleep.

Jar on my grandma's windowsill, little bottles
of insulin in the fridge. When Gary visits, he says after

the accident, an angel brought him back. *I was dead,*
he remembers this, *but it's not like people say.*

Sweetbreads are neither bread nor sweet.

# HARP

The evening seethes with sound, these
cicadas in the trees—

mad thrum of seventeen years underground,
chewing darkness, chewing roots, let loose and out now, singing—

great choruses of them.
Joyce's boy says his body is a harp, and every word

his buddy's sister says is a finger running on the wires.
I try to remember what that was like,

listening to the plague of locusts, my dad's backyard,
a moment in the sun

then back to his room, the low hum
of the oxygen tank, shuffled feet.

Tuning pins run through me:
twist them to sharpen the pitch of this—

the skin strung across his ribs like wings, twisted pins
staking up the soul's tent,

guy ropes and pegs, or rigging on an empty mast, the boat going
nowhere, adrift.

I drag behind me a drift net, a croker sack of dead things,
and our phones

are black bugs in our pockets, our hands,
trembling, singing—not yet knowing what the song means.

# THE RAPTURE
*21 May 2011*

I.


Trumpet flower on the ditch, orange blare of blossom over dark
water, over the snake that traces the edge of what we know.

II.


On TV they say the world
will end today,
some preacher has the news,

but I walk the perimeter
of eave and soffit anyway
to zap the carpenter bees,

the ones emerging
from the bored wood,
the ones that hover

all around the house,
bothered, like fat
black angels.

# MOUSETRAPS

The second time my dad decided to die,
we didn't know but thought we knew

better, his vital signs said otherwise,
and he'd done it before, this decision—

his breathing difficult so must be time
to say goodbye. We gathered round his bed,

Jeff and I on either side, my mom
sitting on the bed. We prayed, he asked

if this is how it ends, told us, *I hope
you won't have too big a job cleaning me up.*

Then Aunt Elaine got there, told him to get up
out of that bed, and when he just looked sad, said

*I bet you'll be one bossy angel.* We laughed,
I made some coffee, we settled in for another

night of talking round his bed, watched
the anxiety meds take effect, and later,

when Jeff and Elaine left, I set some mousetraps
round the house before we went to bed.

# MY FATHER AS HARRY HOUDINI

*for Jeff*

This is serious business.
He tucks the pills under his tongue.

His watch falls off, lost in the sheets.
The truck's tailgate won't open.

*There's a trick to it*, my brother says,
showing me how to use a rubber hose

to keep the toolbox closed in case of rain.
*There's a trick to everything around here.*

A key is hidden somewhere on his body.
We wait to see what he will do.

# DISAPPEARING

My father is the disappearing man.
His voice gets smaller and smaller,

though his bones refuse,
and the tumors.

His hands are large, his teeth, too.
It hurts him to turn over.

My mother leans over his bed
to listen to his whisper.

Every morning the curtains open,
the sun colors in his small face.

# LIMINAL

He stands, hesitant,
afraid to interrupt

something, or someone,
his face a thin slate of need

and fear—the way
the open hand is raised

at the jamb, open
to the dark threshold, the other

hand not clutching,
softly touching the gray wall

where he pauses.
Is it fear—or love? A shadow

draws the throat, limns
the wall behind him.

What is the light that glows
beyond us,

less near and yet nearer,
and nothing we imagine?

# REEF

In the dark, the hospice oxygen tank bubbles like an aquarium,
and in the blue light of their room, my father lies on a narrow reef

of bed. For so long I thought he was a shark—driven thing,
all sharp teeth and short vision. But now I know better, his eyes

closed, dentures too big. He's a diver, hooked to that tank,
about ready to surface, but not yet, my mother in her chair,

leaning on his bed, asleep, this last thing, this anchor.

# KNOWLEDGE

The nurse called it a roller coaster, this lift
and dip of days, the way my father may drift
asleep, twitch and shake, eyes glazed, then wake,
spend the day or night alert. Sometimes

we think it must be the end, but then he's back,
hungry, demanding something sweet, or to be
wheeled out for a smoke, his eyes bright,
that grin. She says he's done this so much

that when it really does get bad, we won't
know to know it, or won't accept that this
is it—expectant, waiting for him to wake,
my mother ready to cook him anything,

and me, ready to lift him to his chair,
wheel him anywhere.

# IT WON'T BE LONG NOW

*17 June 2011*

My mom rubs lotion on his nose, so the mask
won't rub, where it does, because of how he breathes

now. The world is muffled, nothing matters but this,
but him. We tug the blanket to his chin. Outside

it's bright, a haze of heat and light, though here, in here
with him, it's cool, dim. We leave the curtains open

in case he turns to see—we're almost there, the day
the sun stands still, the year's hinge, each day longer

than before—it won't be long now, the storms
whipping the weeds along the ditch, the road, and somewhere

a shining line of blue, a door open, a crack.
It's what we know is true, but don't yet say, can't.

# THE LANGUAGE OF FLANNELGRAPH

*Beedeville Church of Christ, Vacation Bible School, July 1980*

I.

A sheep and a goat is Jacob and Esau. A sheep
and a goat and angel with trumpet is the end of things.

Put the goat on the left, sheep on the right.

A pair of animals means flood or garden—depends
if you want to destroy it all or save it. Or name it.

II.

The robed man who stands is father, is lord,
is Abraham, is Isaac, is Jacob, is Moses, is prophet,

is wiseman, is priest, is depends-on-the-story, what's needed.

The kneeling man is son, is leper, is servant,
is Esau, is Saul, is penitent, is lost—lost son,

lost coin, lost lamb—or for the parable of talents.

III.

Don't lose the burning bush, the box of coins,
the tablets of stone, the coat of many colors.

Pigs mean: prodigal son or the legion of demons.
A pair of men can be a healing, one standing,

one kneeling; with the right figures, anything's a miracle.

# - III -

## IN MY FATHER'S HOUSE

# WORTHY

*reading Matthew 8-10*

I.

The multitudes—
and this frenzy of healings, waves of people washing against him,
so many, their hands, their trembling limbs, their lame and crippled
        bodies arranged

on blankets or beds, makeshift litters and carts, their eyes
gummed shut with blindness, tongues dumb clappers in mouths without song,
minstrels keening a dead girl, the crush of people, the noise of their grief,

a man with lesions, the stench of him, a woman sticky with blood—
the text the tale of it thick with seizures and demons, with *divers diseases
and torments*—and his hands everywhere

on sick bodies, dead ones, touching them, the fevered and leprous,
the dead girl, in their rooms, at their deathbeds, touching them,
but not that one—

foreigner, stranger—not that one, the soldier saying, *Lord, I am not worthy
that you should come under my roof*, sick man in the distance, and here
the soldier, subaltern, beseeching,

a man who loved his—*speak the word only*—
a man who loved his servant his son his companion his boy, and, no,
he didn't touch him, not that one, just said so,

and it was so, the way words do things, and the man went on his way, and
the scripture swerves for a little sermon—*That many shall come from the east
and the west and shall sit down with Abraham and Isaac*—that story,

the devout surely taken aback because those they all along thought wrong
are numbered in this little song of fathers and sons, this little lesson
on reconciliation,

though the teacher later said,
*I am come to set a man against his father*—but not *his* father,
who counts the dead birds, who watches them fall, who weighs them

in his hand and says two dead sparrows are worth some money, but not
much, and I think about the dead bird in the yard last spring, not a bird
        really
but a wing, dead thing left by the cat, flat fan spread

in the dirt, now tucked under the roots of a tree
I planted while my father lay dying inside, not long after we'd brought
        him home,
my mom's Arbor Day saplings in the stack of backed up mail.

II.

*If a house be worthy, let your peace come upon it.*
So Jesus was moved to compassion, himself

without home, without foxhole or nest, just a bunch of men
on a ship with him, in a tempest, and no one,
at that moment, believing.

# MY FATHER'S HOUSE

I. *This is the body*

Sundays someone always stops by
with the traveling show of crackers
and magic juice, the shuffle of little cups
from a Ziploc bag—Lord's Supper
for the shut-ins, *the sick and afflicted*
as they say in the ministry lingo.
They left behind the empty cups.
Washed up, they nest on my dresser,
hold the moment when together
we had prayer over my father's bed
about flesh and blood
and something I'm not sure
I still believe—though I believe
in this: five people around a bed,
something shared,
a broken body, bowed heads.

II. *after the Our Father*

Father, lying in that narrow bed,
I am listening for my name.
We know what is coming,
we know what needs to be done
here, now—and later, when you're finally okay.

Mornings, I give you your daily meds.
Please forgive me all that needs forgiven,
as I keep forgiving you.
Later I'll wheel your chair outside
for fresh air and a cigarette,
this simple thing you want.

# THAT DAY

He'd stopped responding, his body
no longer him. We watched for signs—

the ones in the blue book with the ship
sinking on the cover, but nothing

beyond the too-regular gasp of breathing,
one hand swollen, propped on a pillow.

We ate our lunch; nothing was real.
There were no signs. His body

was him and he was his body, thin,
immobile, still breathing, shitting.

We lifted him with the sheet to change
him, my brother holding it while

my mother and I cleaned
him up, apologizing.

That day, we were waiting,
my mother going through a basket

of mail on her bed, turning her head
for a moment, and when she turned

back, my dad had stopped breathing.
It was just like that. He stopped.

And the sun still shining, my brother
on the mower in the back yard,

me kneeling, weeding a flower bed
in the thick heat, picking, then,

at that moment, a tick off my arm.

# "OUT OF THE STRONG CAME FORTH SWEETNESS"

The tunnels stuffed with beebread,
bees hum at soffit and eaves, the soft cedar.

Here he is, breathing, *here.*

Tunnels seethe with feeding,
with pupae, with molting, what will emerge.

That afternoon, already gone.

Will emerge summer's end,
black swarms for the last nectars.

The machine breathes in the dark room.

The lawn shivers, brown leaves lift
and scatter, skitter of brown winged things.

In the story, rotting meat, and sweet.

Small stand against them, this soapy bucket
tucked in zinnias, this sweet trap.

In the story, dead lion, a sheet of bees lifting.

Green snake threads the dead grass.
Bug bucket's sticky with dead things.

In the story, hands full of honey.

A woman at the bed, knows already, but—
Outside, mower, sound of bees, the machine

still breathes in the dark room.

# STOP

*Father's Day, 18 June 2011*

My mom's alarm goes off, beeps
louder and louder and she sleeps on

as my brother goes in and turns it off.
The wheelchair, bedside commode are near

the door for equipment pickup later
this morning. There's a cooler of drinks

a cousin brought last night, the ice
settling, ready for relatives, visitors

we expect all day, today.
Even now, the air conditioner

has stopped, the coffee pot has stopped,
done, the mockingbird outside

the front window has stopped singing.

# GRIEF

Brown thread, white thread:
stitch and unstitch the shock,

able to sense little, sense enough.
Grief is a private religion

of color and touch.
Not then, not time enough, just

now, the warm second.
Touch the animal:

your own hand moving.
See the bones in your own fingers.

# BEFORE THE VIEWING

He seems so small, his hands folded, his suit
a little loose despite the pins and tucks,
the makeup a little too much, his cheeks
pink, his lips. The funeral director adjusts

the lights a little, the pink and blue, but still
he looks like a doll, not a farmer,
not a dead man, not my father. It's difficult
to think here, outside the box.

The director sits with my mother and me
on a pale sofa across the room while one
of her men fusses over him with brush
and tint, browns the lips a bit. She tells

my mother she seems very calm. She is very calm.
We wonder if he should have his glasses on.

# SPINOZA WAS WRONG ABOUT SADNESS

*on learning, after his death, that my father invented*
*a mechanical fruit harvester*

Not much has changed in the past.
What I don't know

are the geographic boundaries.
Rather than the cinderblock apartments,

the sidewalk out front, the sun.
I don't know what he lost,

just that it was stolen from him,
precise diagrams for a harvest machine.

Decades later, he published something
in a magazine of farm implements

and inventions, a description
of a stripper-header device.

Rather than language enriching us,
it rebuilds the gravel road,

the ditch, the empty fields,
a chest filled with correspondences,

sometimes the anthropological gaze.
I imagine the machine's fingers

grooming the trees.

# DEADHEADING

*September 2011*

Deadheading the zinnias that morning, you see it—
coiled there on a small rock, golden brown, its tail

tipped with almost-green, a shiver of color.

Your brother says if you see one, you'll see more.
Your cousin says the little ones are the deadliest.

You go inside for your camera, snap it
for posting later, after you've killed it,

after you've sliced off its flat and golden head
with a shovel, its thin dead coil on the lawn,

after you've raked the bed for its brothers.

When you lift it, sluggish, from the bed,
lean close to its dappled slither. Your father

never brought it up again after that one time
when you first got back, the man you left

at home, all that, though you knew
the bite of it was still there

at the back of his throat, on the tip
of his dry tongue, the teeth

he could put back in.

# THIRST

The nurse said, your father really looks at you
when you walk into the room—

he stares at you,
she said, he must have something to tell you.

But he never tells you.

Later, another hospice worker listened to this story.
She said, no, you know,

sometimes, as we're leaving this world,
our world contracts to the small space of the room,

to the few things we love.

Your father wasn't looking at you because he had
something to tell you, no,

he was looking at you because he loved you, she said.
It was near the end, she said,

he was drinking you in.

# HOUSESHOES

Two woodpeckers worry the dogwood limbs,
tugging on the red berries, making
a noise like gurgling, a burble of hunger song,
the cat in the window, twitching with it.

Two men walk the yard, making decisions,
making decisions about will and testament
and the amaryllis left out for the cold,
what will come back, what won't, and who.

The air is filled with leaves rotting, a faint
smell of human sewage, someone's septic
system backed up, the creek down the street
shriveling dry. The sun is heavy on its

tether. One man has on houseshoes.
He's been in them all day.

# DECEMBER

*for Bert*

After four warm days in December
and another gazania blooming out front,
nothing makes sense, the sad year

almost gone. This may be a love poem.
All the fields are filled with sadness,
or something like sadness, a hardening.

I dreamed last night the sky was filled
with stars, and I tried to point out
a falling star to you, its surge of beauty,

and I dreamed my mother was running,
best she could, toward a glass door
at the end of a long hallway, and it was

bright outside, beyond the door, and she
knew, that there, out there, she would
be healed. I woke up crying.

# PARK

*Dublin, winter 2011*

Rain in the park, near dark, the trees
leaning over the wet walks,

bark washed slick and black, the leaves
a pale gold, glowing, cold,

and the faint smell here of something
sour, the pond funky with ducks

and gulls, mounded leaves moldering,
and my heart, here, far

from home, thick with memories of my father,
those last moments. It's not

that things had to be said—the dead
keep speaking after all—just

how quietly they speak,
how quietly.

# LIGHT

Two black dogs eat something dead
in the middle of the stubbled field.

The field is empty. The dogs pause
to watch cars drive by, turn back to the dark

carcass, hidden in the stalks, last year's
harvest. The field is not empty: it is full

of light. The dogs eat what they find.
I can barely see them in the rearview mirror.

The sun spreads its cold and careless light
across the sky, the fields, the lonely road.

# WHEN I OPEN MY MOUTH TO ASK FOR FORGIVENESS

When I open my mouth to ask for forgiveness,
an armadillo crawls out, all armor and claws,
ready to curl up into an impenetrable ball,
ready to claw whatever gets too close.
It is hungry for something dug up, something
helpless and white, dug out of the dark.

When I open my mouth to ask for forgiveness,
a rose of Sharon blooms, opening its lavender
and white petals, hiding my face.
The armadillo digs a den beneath the roses.

When I open my mouth to ask for forgiveness,
a snake comes out. It crawls across the yard
and up the front wall and into a window, the gap
between pane and screen, where it will be
seen from inside the front room, where my nephews
are hitting each other, my mother pretending
to listen to my niece, really listening for my father.
Someone will see it, someone will kill it,
someone will sever its head, the body flopping
like a bit of black rope on the front lawn,
something glistening, something unbound.
The armadillo has dug up the zinnias, looking
for grubs, the flowers splayed, faded.

When I open my mouth to ask for forgiveness,
a little boy crawls out. He wanders off
down the ditch bank, collecting pretty things—
seedpods, goldenrod, buckeyes, anything
that catches his eye. I hope he'll come back
before dark. My mother says someone
at church saw a panther on the road one night.
There are wolves—she's seen them—in the fields.

When I open my mouth to ask for forgiveness,
a black bee flies out, and then another, carpenter,
harbinger. They fill the eaves, the soft cedar soffits
drilled, tunneled with eggs. Next year maybe,
a dark halo of humming things. Next spring,
next summer, the house hemmed in
by the hover of black wings.

When I open my mouth to ask for forgiveness,
a man crawls out. He is my dead father.
He can walk now, now that it's all over.
He looks at my mother. No one says a word.

# DOGWOOD

The heat comes on, a rumble in the guts of the house,
the unit out back steaming in the cold air.

I've become resistant to apparitions, to those lucent
moments between one darkness and another—

the shepherds leaning on their staffs, scanning the stars.

This year, we brought the plants in before the frost.
We waited too late last year, and the jade tree

that had bloomed before, in the warmth, bloomed
instead with rime, its limbs succulent mush.

Nothing to do but throw it away.
I'm no longer a child, but still—

those winter constellations of pink flowers.

In the unoccupied air of the dark hallway, my father appears.
He says nothing, just watches.

I think my dead father is learning to love me.
Or am I learning to love him.

I've waited a long time for this.

The sun lights up the last leaves of the dogwood
like so many bloody baubles.

# ARK

## NOTES

"Adrift off the Islets of Langerhans" and "How to lift him" were written after reading Ross Gay's "How to fall in love with your father," from *Against Which* (Cavankerry, 2006).

"Home" and "December" are for Bert Easter, who said, *you should stay*.

"Instructions" and "Mousetraps" are for Elaine Thomas.

"Easy" is for Suzanne Madden Hutchinson.

"Black tape" and "My father as Harry Houdini" are for my brother, Jeff Madden.

"When I open my mouth to ask for forgiveness" begins with a line adapted from "Sin and Forgiveness" by Zachary Schomburg, from *Scary, No Scary* (Black Ocean, 2009).

"It won't be long now" was written in response to a painting of that title by Lee Monts, from a series of paintings about his father's death.

# ACKNOWLEDGMENTS

Grateful acknowledgment is made to the editors of the following publications in which these poems first appeared, some in slightly different versions:

*Arkansas Review*: "Flood," "Field guide, after the floods," and "Landscape, with levees"

*Assaracus*: "Deadheading"

*Chelsea Station Magazine*: "When I open my mouth to ask for forgiveness"

*Crannóg* (Ireland): "Song" and "Rain" (published together as "Hospice")

*Crazyhorse*: "Thirst"

*Cross Currents: Journal of Religion and Intellectual Life*: "The rapture" and "My father's house"

*Cyphers* (Ireland): "Grief"

*Good Men Project*: "When my father woke"

*Image*: "Fist" and "The language of flannelgraph"

*Iodine Poetry Journal*: "December"

*The Journal of the South Carolina Medical Association*: "Instructions," "Knowledge," and "Reef" (as "Anchor") published together as "Thirteen Weeks"

*Ladowich*: "Spinoza was wrong about sadness"

*Los Angeles Review*: "Light"

*MiPoesias*: "Troubling the water" and "Dogwood"

*Natural Bridge*: "Footnote on the Islets of Langerhans"

*The New Guard*: "Adrift off the Islets of Langerhans"

*Poetry at Round Top* (2012): "It won't be long now"

*A Poetry Congeries, Connotation Press:* "After long silence"

*Poetry Ireland Review*: "Ark"

*Poetry Society of South Carolina Yearbook* 2012: "Before the viewing" and "That day"

*Prairie Schooner*: "Because" and "Worthy"

An earlier version of "The house and the surrounding fields" appears in *Found Anew: Poetry and Prose Inspired by the South Caroliniana Library Digital Collections* (USC Press, 2015). It was also published with illustration by Rachel Parker for the Columbia Broadside Project (2014).

"Last night" was published on *What Jasper Said*, the blog of *Jasper: The Word on Columbia Arts*.

"How to lift him" was included in *The Art of Healing*, a book accompanying the Art of Healing gallery show at Tapp's Art Center, Columbia, SC, organized by Jim Dukes in fall 2013. "Going through photos with my mom" (part 1 of "Resemblances") was published in *The Collective I*, a chapbook edited by Susan Levi-Wallach to accompany the "Selfies: Real or Imagined" show at Gallery West, West Columbia, spring 2015.

"My father's house" (as "Poem from my father's house") and "Landscape with levees" are included in the essay "*Scientia mortis* and the *ars moriendi*: to the memory of Norman," by Jeffrey Bishop, in the *Health Humanities Reader* (Rutgers, 2014).

"How to lift him," "Knowledge," and "Thirst" were incorporated into the Ted talk "How to lift him," presented at the TedX conference in Columbia, SC in 2014 (http://tedxtalks.ted.com/video/How-to-lift-him-Ed-Madden-at-TE).

I am deeply grateful to Ron Mohring and Seven Kitchens Press, who published earlier versions of several of these poems in the chapbook *My Father's House* (2013). I am also deeply grateful to Patrick Dover, who set that chapbook to music for an orchestral and choral performance in late 2013.

Deepest thanks to Kwame Dawes, Ray McManus, and Daniel Nathan Terry, who read these poems in manuscript, and to Ray for the pints and encouragement. Thanks as well to Bryan Borland and Sibling Rivalry Press, to John Lane for his extraordinary book *The Dead Father Poems*, and to Bert Easter, first and dearest reader. For their friendship, support, and inspiration, special thanks to Nathalie Anderson, Jennifer Bartell, Cindi Boiter, Jack Brannon, Betsy Breen, Josh Brewer, Greg Brownderville, Darien Cavanaugh, Melissa Dugan, Josh English, D. Gilson, Kathryn Kirkpatrick, Etta Madden, Suzanne Madden Hutchinson, Ray McManus, Susan Laughter Meyers, Lee Monts, Nekki Shutt, Lee Snelgrove, Elaine Thomas, Barbara Thomson, Dan Vera, William Wright, and Ivan Young.

Finally, in so many ways, this book is for my mother, the strongest woman I know.

# ABOUT THE POET

Born and raised in rural Arkansas, Ed Madden teaches at the University of South Carolina. He is the author of three previous books of poetry—*Signals* (USC, 2008), which won the South Carolina Poetry Book Prize, *Prodigal: Variations* (Lethe, 2011), and *Nest* (Salmon, 2014). His poems have appeared in *Prairie Schooner, Crazyhorse, Poetry Ireland Review*, and other journals, as well as in *Best New Poets 2007, The Book of Irish American Poetry*, and *Hard Lines: Rough South Poetry*, and online at the *Good Men Project*. In 2015 he was named the poet laureate for the City of Columbia, South Carolina.

# ABOUT THE PRESS

Sibling Rivalry Press is an independent press based in Little Rock, Arkansas. Its mission is to publish work that disturbs and enraptures. This book was published in part due to the support of the Sibling Rivalry Press Foundation, a non-profit private foundation dedicated to assisting small presses and small press authors.

CPSIA information can be obtained at www.ICGtesting.com
Printed in the USA
LVOW10s0449130416

483328LV00009B/116/P